YOUR KNOWLEDGE HAS VALUE

Gebhard Deissler

Respecting Foreigners

GRIN Publishing

Bibliographic information published by the German National Library:

The German National Library lists this publication in the National Bibliography;
detailed bibliographic data are available on the Internet at http://dnb.dnb.de .

Imprint:

Copyright © 2010 GRIN Verlag, Open Publishing GmbH
Print and binding: Books on Demand GmbH, Norderstedt Germany
ISBN: 978-3-640-79470-6

This book at GRIN:

http://www.grin.com/en/e-book/159901/respecting-foreigners

GRIN - Your knowledge has value

Since its foundation in 1998, GRIN has specialized in publishing academic texts by students, college teachers and other academics as e-book and printed book. The website www.grin.com is an ideal platform for presenting term papers, final papers, scientific essays, dissertations and specialist books.

Gebhard Deißler

RESPECTING

FOREIGNERS

CULTURE RESEARCH
KULTUR FORSCHUNG
RECHERCHE CULTURE
BUSQUEDA CULTURAL
RICERCA CULTURALE

RESPECTING FOREIGNERS

The following exposé is largely based on the following I-We-They Principle, which refers to the perception of oneself, one's own cultural group as well as that of other cultural groups:

- "I am complex, three dimensional and flexible – able to operate with a full range of behaviour according to the context
- **WE** are less complex, two dimensional – operating within a narrower range of predictable behaviours
- **THEY** are simple, one dimensional – operating within clearly identifiable and narrow behaviours."

(International Management Training Package, World Work Ltd, London)

Perceived distance and complexity condition our thinking and feeling about people from other cultures. Greater distance, lesser complexity and negative judgement correspond and smaller distance, greater complexity and positive judgements also go hand in hand. In the above summary of the I-We-They principle in three categories the We refers to the cultural group of the I, while They corresponds to members of other cultural groups with differing value preferences from oneself and one's own cultural group.

The term foreigner already implies a prejudice, a clear-cut categorization and antagonization of people from different parts of the world. The use of the term "people from other countries" reduces the distance, appreciates their being humans by calling them people. They are put on an equal footing with natives who are also people, from diverse places as well. The ensuing reduction of distance increases their complexity and humanity, while the term foreigner puts them at a greater distance while it reduces their complexity. The increase of distance reduces their complexity and their humanity with its feelings, emotions, thought, hopes, loves, fears and sorrows. If we strip them of those essential human qualities they appear simple, outsiders and wrong with regard to our map of the world with its differing values, beliefs, assumptions and behaviours. We quickly put an oversimplified label on them to make them more easily manageable in our perception and in actual relationships. We have the right to be here, our norms are accepted, validated, daily reinforced and enforceable. They are simple, wrong and can only hope to be tolerated as marginals, who do not have the same legitimacy, no right to be here, except for what they contribute perhaps as foreign workers. This perception is intensified when we not only reduce their complexity, but when they additionally come with weak educational backgrounds not infrequently close to analphabetism, not knowing the local language and therefore being defenseless. If they additionally come from socioeconomically disadvantaged backgrounds and without urban sophistication it increases their simplicity. So we strip them of their complex humanity, put a label of tolerated simplicity on them and treat them as foreigners instead of people with equal rights and duties. This is a tendency, not the rule and some people from other countries may not always deserve an equal or preferential treatment. But this is as exceptional the preferential treatment is. The distance at which we put the foreigners may be a normal or bell curve distribution, a variation around a mean like many social statistical phenomena: a minority may put them at a small distance, a majority at quite a distance due to their perceived forcignness with regard to values and behaviours and another minority may put them at a great distance in order to handle them more easily as marginals, because they may appear unworthy, a threat or as competitors for the same share of the cake, however, with less legitimacy.

If increased perceived distance reduces complexity of people and categorizes them as out-group and wrong, the reverse process should also apply in view of the harmonization and normalization of intercultural relations. How can that approach

3

to improved intercultural understanding and cooperation be implemented practically?

I have just returned from shopping and I did not really see a way to continue what I yesterday considered a topic worth writing about, as we are surrounded by a high level of domestic interculturalism, Asian, EU, Eastern European, African etc. The city I live in has the highest percentage of foreigners in the entire country; up to 50 % among the young.

However, I was inspired at the grocery shop at a great distance from my place of residence where I go myself now and then to revive old relationships which date back to my adolescence and which help me now and then to retune my relationship with the local culture when I have been travelling a lot intellectually or physically. Anyhow, I observed the following real life example of decreasing distance and increasing complexity, which seemed to have a satisfactory effect on the interactants: The transaction between the cashier and the foreign woman with a little girl, probably her daughter went far beyond the fairly anonymous standard business transaction of money for goods. They moved from transaction to interaction in spite of the poor linguistic capabilities of the foreign lady who could only talk the non-verbal language of softness and smiles compared to the cashier. The cahier addressed the little girl of pre-school age about the kindergarten she went to (apparently there was a previous exchange on the topic which she resumed). I did not hear a single word uttered by the two foreign persons. But judging from the satisfaction and the smiles, I concluded that it was an interaction, which not only broke the ice and showed care and concern by resuming a thread of communication. The distance was decreased and the complexity and humanity of the non locals increased by not only treating them as clients but by also inquiring non-inquisitively about other aspects relating to the kindergarten. That also confirmed and valued the woman indirectly as not only a customer but also as a mother. The mother and the daughter felt that they were seen and appreciated as persons with various facets, multidimensionally and were therefore confirmed in their humanity and multi-layered identity. So, here decrease of distance through increase of complexity led not only to an effective transaction but also to a seemingly satisfactory intercultural interaction. If this threat of communications is maintained along with a positive kindergarten experience of cultural adaptation and integration together with other positive feedback, the feeling of acceptance in the local community and therefore the integration process as a whole can work out as it should.

As examples are more educational than theoretical considerations I would like to illustrate the process once more by drawing on my personal experience: A few years ago I volunteered as honorary secretary of the Spanish Library Association. I proposed to the Spanish steering committee a fundraising campaign in order to acquire literature intended for the members of the local Spanish community (colonia). The literature was intended to satisfy the cultural needs of the members of the colony and to maintain the cultural connection with the home culture, to which many of them might return one day after a working life abroad. It can also provide a resource to transmit the cultural-linguistic heritage and identity to the next generation of immigrants and to foster a bicultural identity.

So I wrote a letter to the major local global corporations asking for a donation for this purpose. The response was positive, which showed the members of the Spanish community that they were not only appreciated as so-called foreign labour but also as human beings with cultural needs. Not only the concern of the corporations materializing as financial donations but also my personal commitment free of charge to their cause further confirmed their cultural identity and their diverse aspects and needs as members of the local culture. The campaign required regular meetings and cooperation which involved interaction in a wide spectrum of issues. Progressively the constructive commitment and support in a foreign cultural environment evolved into friendship and mutual support.

Material cooperation and friendship involve the full complexity of a person, distance ceases, there is no I nor We nor They left, no barrier, but only relationship based on empathy and reciprocity which extended beyond library issues. I experienced it, and I hope my Spanish friends for whom it probably was a vital concrete and symbolical integration experience, as a process which respected and even transcended cultural issues altogether, as a good relationship among people in which diversity was appreciated and valued.

Sensitivity to the totality of a foreign person's needs can initiate processes of very successful interaction, acceptance and integration. First, one has to allow people to enter one's perception, recognize them for what they are, respect them with their needs and find ways to meet such needs. The process of recognizing, respecting and catering for such needs – if applicable – progressively reduces distance, while it increases complexity and results in successful intercultural interaction. In the context of an acculturation process it will speed up and consolidate the process and finally result in solidarity with the host country culture and its members. Otherwise they might remain aliens, who make their living in the host country but - beyond this - remain marginals, suspended between diverse cultures, without a real home. They had to leave one home for economic reasons and the host country could not provide a replacement for the lost home. Through successful acculturation they can regain aspects of their familiar home country paradise lost to use a literary analogy.

Otherwise they might remain uprooted in a no man's land between cultures and silently oppose the local culture because deep down they might have a feeling of a (collective) persona non grata except for their working contribution. Acceptance by the host country culture members leads to real acceptance of the local culture by the immigrants. Mutual acceptance results in more complex and richer relationships, where all sorts of cultural and linguistic, educational, racial barriers etc. can be bridged, because a general mindset of goodwill prevails. Ticking time bombs, the extreme opposite of perceived cultural integration, as happened in England and not only there, should be quasi impossible in such a context, because the prevailing spirit of proactive integration is stronger than the sword of discord. Such thoughts would be part of a blue print for an integration agenda.

Integration policy makers in Europe, in England, Germany, Spain and France should find out to what extent they can reduce the distance with regard to their culturally more distant Muslim immigrant community among other immigrants in order to defuse ticking time bombs which result from the cultivation of distance, which reduces them to scapegoats and marginalizes them. Not accepting and confirming their identity as members of one or more cultures – depending on the generational genealogy – and as human beings with their universal and special cultural needs breeds resentment, resistance and rebellion. They should neither be treated as princes nor as pariahs, but as human beings with their rights and duties, as any citizen of the planet without distinction between natives and foreigners in line with local and international law. As diverse members of the same humanity they are entitled to the same rights and privileges as any member of that humanity. All civilized constitutions of the earth, in particular those of immigration countries par excellence like Canada and the USA among others underline that all men are born equal. But it took more than 300 years to honour such lofty assumptions, even though they are carved in stone and although they can be enforced legally.

Man's mind is indeed slow to change but the universal process of awareness building of diversity issues will surely receive momentum in the third millennium total integration of the global village we inhabit. The multi-factored complexity of the earth with its entire biosphere as well as the multidimensional complexity of its inhabitants, humans and other creatures, will be put before men's eyes. No one will be able to put himself at an unattainable distance to the totality of the existential complexity of maybe soon a dozen billion culturally diverse people on a single planet without alternative and escape route.

This perspective requires multidimensional management of complexity at the individual, organisational, national and global level; the need for an enhanced UN Charter, institutions and policy and empowerment, if the emerging global complexity is to be managed successfully. And the management of such complexity needs concomitantly more global as well as more local approaches. If the national cultural institutional environments cannot manage their complexities how could then complexity at a global scale be managed? In order to succeed in this lofty long-term global scale policy little local steps should be taken as pointed out at the beginning. A successful model in one culture can teach the world best practice.

Maybe man's image of his fellow man needs a revision in light of the imperatives of global magnitude. The major religions and ethical systems should be the torchbearers of a global change of mindset in line with their noblest traditions so as to sustainably impact every corner of the world. Only if man perceives a reflection of the creator in his fellow man irrespective of his cultural and other origins and outer appearances, if he can therefore relate to him at the level which unifies all men and creation, as opposed to the outer appearances and values... which diversify men, an all encompassing human solidarity can be reached which is integrative by nature and will therefore do no harm to any creature, but rather promote them. By promoting them he will realize that he promotes himself, due to the mystical bond of all members of creation. If the concept of the self can be enhanced in this direction all men will be solidary not only among themselves but also with the totality of creation. Certainly that will please the Creator and He will give Hs blessing, leading to the fulfillment of man's mission and existence, individually and as mankind on earth and beyond.

My essay started with the barrier breaking interaction between a cashier and a kindergarten age girl and her mother which is small scale integration. But as a snow flake can in time produce an avalanche, a river become an ocean and as the vibration of the wings of a butterfly can trigger a hurricane, so can large scale integration of nations, continents and the entire earth as whole be reached based on concrete local steps; the reencounter, face-to-face, between the Creator and his Creation, the return to one of what has started as one and which has diversified as a process of evolution. Diversification and the evolution required for the successful integration of this diversity in order to return to one, to unity, were the rationale of the trajectory.

If one expands one's awareness to encompass this supposed rationale, one may derive a deeper understanding of diversity and increased integration capability because it is seen in line with the overall purpose. It makes sense and constitutes the ultimate sense making of culture and cultures. It is diversity management in a cosmic context, the highest possible vantage point one may adopt. This results in extraordinary cultural awareness, knowledge and skills. In light of such awareness all cultural diversity questions subside. They are resolved. They do not surface anymore to create havoc. Here culture ends and with its end cultural problems end. And cultural issues can be classed in the records of man's evolution on earth: the culture file can be closed, the book of diversity put back on the shelf of time.

To conclude I would like to quote a piece of poetry by an Indian mystic poet (Darshan Singh) that captures the spirit of the exposed in inspirational language.

We are but drops in the same fountain

   of divine beauty;

We are but waves

   on the great river of love.

We are diverse blossoms

   in the Garden of the Lord,

Who have gathered

   In the same valley of light.

We who dwell on this earth

   belong one humanity;

There is but one God,

   and we are his children

Let us march forth

   to overcome the storms of strife;

Let us march forth

   to light the lamp of Universal Love.

Let the lotus of renewed aspirations

   blossom in our hearts,

And let those long divided

   embrace on another.

Darshan Singh; Poet, Mystic.